A THOUSAND TIMES EXCITED
OR
NOT EXCITED AT ALL

REV. WILLIAM D. HUTCHINSON

Published by:

Editor: Cleveland O. McLeish (Author C. Orville McLeish)

ISBN: 978-976-96194-7-0 (paperback)
         978-976-96194-8-7 (eBook)

ENDORSEMENT

Bishop William Hutchinson, an accomplished author, explores the origins, manifestations, and consequences of human excitement from a Biblical perspective in his fifth book, **"A Thousand Times Excited Or Not Excited At All."** This book explores the excitements as demonstrated in the different dispensations through theological reflections, historical perspectives, and practical applications. It also highlights the point that even though excitement is a natural part of human emotions and existence, one must seek to create that balance between excitement, wisdom, and obedience, as this will allow us to better understand God's purpose for our lives.

This beautifully written book challenges readers to reflect not only on the power of excitement but also on the responsibilities that come with the choice of excitement in this society of excitement.

I commend Bishop Hutchinson for this bold and insightful move in writing **"A Thousand Times Excited Or Not Excited At All."** It is a timely, relevant, engaging, and thought-provoking read.

Dr. Paulette V. Bryan. J.P
Educator/Lecturer
Minister of Religion

DEDICATION AND ACKNOWLEDGEMENTS

To my late mother, Miss Janet Reid; Sister Janet (Mama) of Marlie Hill, Manchester for my upbringing.

To my dear wife and life partner, Arlene, for helping me stay on the right track.

To my daughter, Karlene, her husband, Mario, and my grandson, Kristoff.

To my daughter, Kadeen, and her four children, Jonathan, Raheem, Kaleica and Mia.

To my sisters, Hermina and Naina, and my brothers, Huglen and Eric.

To my cousin, Leon M. Langley, former minister at the Marlie Hill Church, Manchester Church of God of Prophecy (COGOP), now pastor of the Nomprel Church of God of Prophecy, Manchester, who was the first person to identify the ministerial gifts in me.

To Bishop Ronald J. McFarlane (Former Parish Overseer of Clarendon South and Pastor of the 30A Fernleigh Avenue COGOP, May Pen, Clarendon) who later confirmed the ministerial call on my life.

To my two pastorates, Bustamante Highway and Free Town, COGOP.

To my area of administration, Clarendon South. For their support throughout my ministerial experiences.

ABOUT THE BOOK

There are several schools of thought regarding the excitement in the Garden of Eden when Adam awoke from his sleep and saw the amazing figure—Eve—completely naked. In that moment, he immediately claimed her, saying: **"This is now bone of my bones, and flesh of my flesh; she shall be called Woman, because she was taken out of Man." (Genesis 2:23-KJV).**

One might wonder about Adam's exclamation, his outburst, and his declaration—especially when he had no competitor. Yet, suddenly, he gave her a title (name), "Woman," and proclaimed that she belonged to him: bone of his bones, and flesh of his flesh. This statement implies not just ownership, but also subjection.

The greater significance of the story lies in the question: *Why did they hide after eating the fruit from the middle of the Garden?* They ate it, despite being instructed not to. When God visited them and called out as usual, they excused themselves because they had become aware of their nakedness. They made aprons, not coats, breastplates, hats, or shoes—not full garments that could cover the entire body. Instead, they focused only on covering their groin area.

We will explore this and much more in this thought-provoking book.

TABLE OF CONTENTS

PREFACE

Observation proves that when most men see women, especially their woman—wives, lover, partner—they get excited.

The first time Adam saw his wife, Eve, he got excited, and by inheritance, men are destined to be excited.

There is therefore no question where all this excitement came from. It came from Adam, and we receive it as a part of our inheritance. When God created Adam, He put Eve inside of him, but she was hidden from him, and it remained that way until after an extensive longing for her beyond tolerable levels: a period of yearning and searching for the missing one, the mysterious one, but obviously, Adam just did not know where to find her, then God put him to sleep and took her out of him by a process of separation. When Adam saw Eve, they were both naked and not ashamed, like young children (see Genesis 2:21-25). It was okay because they were both innocent and blameless, and all that happened, in theological terms, during the dispensation of innocence.

Since the end of the **dispensation of innocence,** which is from creation to the fall of Adam, and throughout the other six dispensations, both men and women continue to be excited and increasingly so. Note carefully that during that period of innocence, there was no real need for covering because innocence allowed them to remain naked and in good moral standing.

On reflection, the climatic conditions were either very good or the first man, and the first woman's skin was so strong and resilient that they existed without clothing, allowing Adam and Eve not to need covering until it was time to hide; this was during the **dispensation of conscience.** Adam and Eve discovered that they were both naked, so they hid themselves (see Genesis 3:7-13).

Adam and Eve thought they could hide; that was only an opinion. The fact is, there are two persons we cannot hide from, even if we tried: one is omniscient and omnipresent, and the other has no such power. One is God and the other is yourself. David, the Psalmist, tried it, and it never worked for him; neither will it work for us.

"…the darkness and the light are both alike to thee." (Psalm 139:12 – KJV).

Clearly we can run as much as we want, but we cannot hide from God (see Psalm 139:5-15).

SECTION 1

1. Excitement

2. Where Did All This Excitement Come From?

3. Who Is Behind This Excitement?

4. If There Is No Excitement?

5. Why Are You Not Excited?

CHAPTER 1

EXCITEMENT

Excitement is described by the **Merriam-Webster Dictionary** as *"A feeling of great enthusiasm and eagerness,"* with other synonyms such as:

1. Exhilaration
2. Elation
3. Breathtaking
4. Animation
5. Enthusiasm
6. Eagerness
7. Zeal
8. Zest
9. Vim
10. Spark

Just to mention a few.

The Thesaurus further gives a total of three hundred and fifty eight words, both synonyms and antonyms, that are further grouped for emphasis as follows:

1. **For sexual arousal**: It defines it as passion, attraction, or stimulation.

2. For more-excitement, the "Cambridge Dictionary" lists eleven causes of excitement, as follows:

a) Thrilling events
b) Sensation
c) Public
d) Uproar
e) Stir
f) Commotion
g) To-do
h) Thrill
i) Agitation
j) Hit
k) Scandal

One of the examples that the Cambridge Dictionary gives for excitement is, *"It can make your heart pound, especially when doing somethings for the first time, such as: parachuting, or fighting for the defense of organized religion against its enemies."*

There are other grouped words, such as:

Compared Synonyms:

- Strong matches: 15 examples listed
- Strongest matches: 10 examples listed
- Weak matches: 20 examples listed

Excitement antonyms: Compares the active and the passive modes of excitement in order to kick in the overriding message the word carries:

1. Serenity
2. Peace
3. Inactivity
4. Lethargy
5. Sluggishness
6. Dullness
7. Boredom

The overall state of excitement is beyond ordinary explanation. There are levels of excitement that people crave, which, if not managed, can lead to excitement-burnout, as described by the mental health reference: WebMB as an occurrence that happens to everyone at some point or another. Our lives get busy, and we deal with various responsibilities, be it:

1. Work
2. Helping others
3. Taking care of our families

Sometimes we get so busy we forget to take a step back and rest; that is when **excitement-burnout** can occur. It is a form of exhaustion caused by constantly feeling overwhelmed, and it occurs when we experience excessive emotional, physical, and mental fatigue for an extended period. In many cases, burnout can occur in various areas of life before it impacts our health. It is even worse when one is stressed, depleted, and overwhelmed both physically and mentally. You may not acknowledge or treat it because the condition is not medically diagnosed.

In a biblical context, self-control is referred to as "temperance" or "self-discipline." It is the ability to restrain and govern our thoughts, words, actions, and desires, demonstrating a key virtue and the fruit of the Spirit. Self-discipline should be the driving force behind excitement; therefore, it must be governed by integrity, remaining relevant to the Christian code of conduct and how we manage our excitement.

CHAPTER 2

WHERE DID ALL THIS EXCITEMENT COME FROM?

Regarding the originality and **Adam's** excitement, it is evidenced by his reaction to the responsibilities devolved upon him by the Creator: to have authority over the beasts of the field, the birds of the air, the fish of the sea, and every other thing that creeps on the earth. To name the animals and have over-all command on them. He was also excited to have the privilege to dress and keep the Garden of Eden, and to eat of every tree in the garden that he desired except from the tree in the midst of the garden.

Clearly, the first man had almost enough to excite himself sufficiently, and I think he was, but when he pinned and longed for that which he did not see, the great all-knowing rescued him from all the dangers that were associated with that dimension of longing. The Creator put him to sleep, performed the first surgery, then He presented the first woman to him. He took one woman from one rib and gave her to Adam. Note carefully that Adam had twenty-four ribs, and the Creator took only one. He made only one woman; this is a statement that He intended for a man to have only one woman for life.

When the first man woke up from his sleep and saw Eve, he was so **excited** to see her, the first other human being—a woman—and she was stone-naked; he exclaimed **"This is now bone of my bones,**

and flesh of my flesh: she shall be called Woman." (Genesis 2:23-KJV). Adam had no competitor, no choice, yet he made a declaration that could ward off everyone else: "She is bone of my bone; she is mine!" He was so possessive that he gave her his name, "Wo-Man." I can only imagine the great excitement.

Naturally, every other animal displays this type of prowess for their partner. It is said that males of most animals are more attractive than females, but with humans, females are generally considered more attractive than males.

Examples of male attraction:

- The peacock
- The lion
- The deer
- The snake
- The bluethroat bird
- Fishes
- Dogs
- Cats
- Elephants

That is why Adam was so excited when he saw Eve; she was so beautiful to behold, so he stated his claim with excitement, and it continues from that time to present.

Adam had no other human being to learn how to be possessive, not even another person to make a comparison or to compete with. Obviously, he must have been designed with some degree of excitement. The difference with us today is that we learnt from

Adam that we can make comparisons and, certainly, we have choices.

If we do not coach our children on how to control their attraction or excitement, they are going to get excited, it will happen naturally, because of the original design of the first man.

The prayer of serenity comes into play here, ***"Lord, grant me the serenity to accept the things I cannot change. Courage to change the things I can. And the wisdom to know the difference."***

<h1 style="text-align:center">CHAPTER 3</h1>

<h2 style="text-align:center">WHO IS BEHIND THIS EXCITEMENT?</h2>

The word **excitement** is only found twice in the English Bible: in **Psalm 45:15** *(Easy to Read Version)* and **Psalm 66:6** (*Tyndale Living Bible.*) Another synonym used in this discourse is "delight." Delight it is found **two hundred and sixty-one** times in the **Old Testament and sixty-four times** in the **New Testament** and is associated with the more commonly used word, **joy**. The word "delight" is defined by the American Heritage Dictionary as follows: excitement, great pleasure or significance, joy, something that gives great pleasure or enjoyment, and, as an adjective, "greatly pleasing or delightful."

Humans were made in the image and likeness of God; therefore, it is safe to say God delights in incomparable perfections and glory (see Genesis 1:26-27). We are mostly excited, like Adam, each time we see our partner, our lover, our soulmate, our confidant, our sweetheart because we inherited that trait from Adam. It is the Creator who made us this way.

So, each time we see our partner, we are inclined to play the masculine role. We (men) know we are in charge, therefore, we say kind, sweet and nice things to them, like "You are bone of my bone," meaning, "You are mine." We are inclined to ward-off all suspects, ill-willed and bad-intentioned characters from coming near our significant other. We also know we have a duty to be

23

protective, supportive, kind, compassionate, warm and gentle, in the ways we discharge our duties, similar to the way the first man Adam discharged his.

Men anticipate the **Ephesians 5:22-24** account to always fall into place, **"Wives, submit themselves to your own husbands, as unto the Lord. For the husband is the head of the wife, even as Christ is the head of the Church: and He is the savior of the body. Therefore, as the church is subject to Christ, so let the wives be to their own husbands in everything." (LAB).** This is indeed **exciting** to know, that an instruction was given to first man, and certainly, men in general, have no plan whatsoever to change, adjust, or amend it in any way, shape, or form. For to change that instruction or allow it to be changed, is to give up, compromise or downplay the original procedure that first man was designed to follow.

The Creator is behind all this excitement; as it was in the beginning, so will it be, even to the end of the world. Men must play their masculine roles with excitement on all sides round in order to enjoy the fullness of God's design in the creation of the world. The Creator knew that a life or a relationship without excitement is not going anywhere, because dullness is flatness, dryness, and lacks joy; it is too close to death.

We are fearfully and wonderfully made. We are His people; His children resemble Him as He designed us, just as our offspring resemble us. Realizing this, there is no doubt about who is behind this excitement. It is natural, and should be embraced, but it is also our responsibility to control our reactions and responses when we experience it.

"Nay but, O man, who art thou that repliest against God? Shall the thing formed say to him that formed it, Why hast thou made me thus? Hath not the potter power over the clay, of the same lump to make one vessel unto honour, and another unto dishonour? What if God, willing to shew his wrath, and to make his power known, endured with much longsuffering the vessels of wrath fitted to destruction:" (Romans 9:20-22 – KJV).

When the Creator designed the first man, Adam, He knew the frailties and limitations of man because He is Omniscient. He gave us the opportunity to differentiate between God's perfection and man's imperfection. Man is ever failing, and God is never failing, therefore He deserves to be worshipped.

God is not to be blamed for man's failure. He made us in His likeness, but He gave us a free will, the choice we make in life comes with responsibility.

"Be not deceived; God is not mocked: for whatsoever a man soweth, that shall he also reap." (Galatians 6:7 – KJV).

Let us carefully watch what we sow so that there will be no surprise when reaping time comes. Let us be mindful of ourselves and the lives we live and strive to have control of our excitement.

CHAPTER 4

IS THERE NO EXCITEMENT?

Rarely can men be happy without excitement, according to **Genesis 2:18: "And the Lord God said, It is not good that the man should be alone; I will make him an help meet for him." (KJV).** So, except for a devoted life of chastity or physical incapacity, men should not choose to be alone permanently.

The excitement experienced by men when they encounter women is normal, and it comes naturally, and it is not because one has fallen from grace or lost self-control. For example, every time a man sees a woman, his integrated alert system kicks in, and he becomes aware that she is of a different sex; his mind and body respond to that.

Flee sexual immorality. Every sin that a man does is outside the body, but he who commits sexual immorality sins against his own body. Or do you not know that your body is the temple of the Holy Spirit who is in you, whom you have from God, and you are not your own? For you were bought at a price; therefore glorify God in your body and in your spirit, which are God's. (1 Corinthians 6:18-20 – NKJV).

This applies to both males and females.

Regarding the first man, the Creator said, *"I will make a help meet for him."* This indicates that regardless of one's position or condition, as the old Jamaican proverb says, *"every hoe have their stick a bush"* so clearly, there is a suitable partner for every person, regardless.

This condition applies to all living creatures, regardless of species, sex, social or financial standing, age, culture, appearance, or political or religious beliefs.

— For males as it is for females.
— For black, white or the yellow race.
— For rich, poor and the middle class.
— For the married and the singles.
— For the young, old, or the middle age.
— For Christians and the Non-Christians.
— For the beautiful, the handsome, and those who are difficult to look at.
— For the ministry as well as the Laity.

A thought of evil comes to everyone, regardless of one's Christian commitment, and so self-control is required at all times, but especially in moments of temptation.

For a woman who chooses to be a perpetual virgin, like the Nuns, then **1 Corinthians 7:32-34** account comes into play. This is the case where a woman cares not to be married because she wants to mind the things of the Lord in a devoted way; when compared to minding the things of a husband, then she should be left alone because the married woman seeks to mind the things of her husband, while the unmarried minds the things of the Lord. The difference between a wife and a virgin must be taken into account.

There is a difference between an unmarried woman and a woman who has never been spoken for because integrity comes into play here. Taking that into account, it should not be that one loses her virginity just for the sake of the excitement or at any cost. It is a choice one may live to regret.

In many cases, the choice to remain unmarried is calculated against marrying for better or for worse. It may be better to settle without the excitement than to marry for the excitement and end up settling for the worst in cases where the worst is feared.

Therefore, if people are not excited about the opposite sex, there must be some extreme conditions preventing it, whether spiritually, mentally, emotionally, physically, or physiologically, because the Creator gave the first man, Adam, dominion over his partner, the excitement and desire for the woman. *It is not good that the man should be alone (see Genesis 2:18).* He commissioned the woman's desire towards her husband and declared that he will rule over her. Therefore, regardless of the condition of rulership and subjectivity, her desire for him should remain. It must not be forgotten what the subjectivity of wife to husband means.

People who are not excited about the opposite sex need to be evaluated, either by self and or by others. It may be necessary to seek professional help, guided by the words of God and by benchmarking the Apostle Paul, who was not married. He said he spoke by permission, ***not by authority.***

Note carefully that the scripture places a reasonable amount of weight on marriage when compared to other subjects, hence the importance.

Marriage appears:

— **146** times in the Old Testament
— **40** times in the New Testament,
— **186** times in total.

See some of the important points that the Apostle Paul discoursed below:

1. **"There are different reasons why some men don't marry, some were born without the ability to produce children, others were made that way later in life, and others have given up marriage because of God's kingdom. This is for anyone who is able to accept it." (Matthew 19:12 – ERV).**

2. **"I am not saying you must marry, but you certainly may if you wish." (1 Corinthians 7:6 – TLB).**

3. **"I wish everyone could get along without marring, just as I do, but are not all the same. God gives some the gifts of a husband or wife, and others the gift of being able to stay happily unmarried." (1 Corinthians 7:7 – TLB).**

4. **"But if they cannot contain, let them marry: for it is better to marry than to burn." (1 Corinthians 7:9 – KJV).**

5. **"But be sure in deciding these matters that you are living as God intended, marrying or not marrying in accordance with God's direction and help, and accepting whatever situation God has put you into. This is my rule for all the churches." (1 Corinthians 7:17 – TLB).**

6. **"But and if thou marry, thou hast not sinned; and if a virgin marry, she hath not sinned. Nevertheless such shall have trouble in the flesh: but I spare you." (1 Corinthians 7:28 – KJV).**

7. **"I am saying this to help you, not to try to keep you from marrying. I want you to do whatever will help you serve the Lord best, with a few other things as possible to distract your attention from Him." (1 Corinthians 7:36 – TLB).**

8. **"I will therefore that the younger women marry, bear children, guide the house, give none occasion to the adversary to speak reproachfully." (1 Timothy 5:14 – KJV).**

There will always be excitement, but God intended it to be within the context of marriage or its pursuit; moral principles should guide us, as outlined in Scripture.

The Different Classes Of Men And Their Excitement Reaction

The Dad University says: *"There is not a scientifically recognized classification of men into different 'classes' or 'types,' but some popular cultures use terms like: alpha, beta, gamma, delta, sigma, and omega to describe perceived personality traits or social roles."*

Examining the behaviors, tendencies, and social dynamics, let us define each category. Other researches show over twenty-four other types of men, but we will only examine these six classes:

— **Alpha:** often described as confident, outgoing; a charismatic leader, and enterprising.

— **Beta:** characterized as friendly, reserved, loyal, and collaborative.

— **Gamma:** described as adventurous, eager, aware, and emphatic.

— **Delta:** often depicted as resentful, blaming, and self-sabotaging.

— **Sigma:** seen as likeable and confident, but cunning and calculating.

— **Omega:** A male who is perceived to be weak, mild-mannered, and unimpressive.

These are just terms.

Some people do not get excited about what they see if others are seeing the same person or thing, and nothing is left for the imagination. Rather, their excitement kicks in when the imagination has to work in overdrive, contemplating the outcome. *What is it like, what will it be like?*

The distinct difference between the first man, Adam, and the first woman, Eve, is evident. When he saw her for the first time, he became excited, and at that moment, he exclaimed, *"This is now bone of my bone and flesh of my flesh."* He had no competitor, no competition, no one else to see her from a human perspective; besides that, he was living in the dispensation of innocence. It was not until the dispensation changed from innocence to conscience that he realized that he had an excitement disorder, so he felt ashamed and hid himself.

Some men will get excited on seeing a naked woman, while others may not get excited at all; in this case, they will react differently.

CHAPTER 5

WHY ARE YOU NOT EXCITED?

One's attraction for another person or thing can be gradual or spontaneous. In order for one to be excited about someone or something, there must be focus; whether it is driven by one's appearance, attitude, commitment, warmth, support, or devotion. If or when those are shattered beyond repair, then it can lead to annoyance and disgust and may even kill the God-given affection you once had.

For excitement to thrive, it must be consistently maintained; even when things go wrong, help can be sought. Christians, especially, know how to forgive, drop charges, give others a chance to make amends, or make adjustments where possible, and help lift them from a place of lowliness to a higher place.

The Thesaurus defines excitement as follows: eagerness, pleasure or exhilaration; it is supported by scriptures in the form of an instruction. Loneliness was forbidden, and help was given to Adam by the Creator, the great all-knowing (see Genesis 2:18). **Song of Solomon 7:10** says, **"I am my beloved's, and his desire is toward me." (KJV).** If that focus on you is not welcomed, then it is unlikely that there will be any excitement at all.

We need to look at some of the reasons why some persons are not at all excited.

Excitement can be driven by the following:

1. Good communication.
2. Giving or receiving support.
3. Maintain commitments.
4. Being emotional.
5. Being responsible.
6. Being understanding.
7. Making oneself understandable.
8. Being forgiving.
9. Being helpful.
10. Being caring.
11. Being warm.

The lack of one of the above points, or a combination of some or all, is enough to kill excitement and bury it without any hope of a resurrection.

Excitement can be fickle; therefore, it must be treated with the highest regard, or else, when we think that excitement is alive, we discover that it is dead. There is also a tendency to pass on our worst traits, and because behavior is learned, the aptitude and attitude to adopt these bad traits may also be learned by others.

Some of the things that prevent people from sharing in the excitement are:

- Selfishness
- Unkindness (mean)
- Impatience.
- Being uncaring

- Being untrusting
- Being too private
- Being irresponsible

Those who possess the good traits mentioned above will be helped, while those who choose the bad will be destroyed. They can certainly make us into characters we did not intend to be and can easily strike the fatal blow to the excitement with which they were created. The positive and negative points outlined above are key factors in determining whether a relationship is better or worse when viewed in the context of marriage.

Some people face disappointments in their marriage. Many people naively think that marriage will solve all their problems. Here are some problems that marriage will not solve:

1. Loneliness
2. Sexual temptation
3. Satisfaction of one's deepest emotional needs
4. Elimination of life's difficulties[1]

Marriage alone does not hold two people together, but commitment does—commitment to Christ and to each other, despite conflicts and problems. As wonderful as marriage is, it does not automatically solve every problem.

Whether married or single, we must be contented with our situation and focus on Christ, not our loved ones, to help address our problems.

---

[1] 1 Corinthians 7:28 LAB Commentary

We should seek to give more than we expect to receive; in giving lies the greater blessing. Let us do all we can to make our lives and the lives of others exciting. It is the ideal situation that God designed for humans to enjoy.

SECTION 2

CHAPTER 6

HOW IT ALL BEGAN

Everything, whether great or small, has a beginning; the only exception is eternity. In the beginning, God created the heavens and the earth in six days; on the sixth day of creation, He made man. It was evident that all the other creatures had companions but poor man (Adam) had none. He soon recognized the need for companionship, which was the very reason for the Genesis 2:18 account. The Creator made man in the likeness and image of Himself, but of his kind, he was alone.

The Creator, the omniscient, the all-wise, responded to Adam's unspoken request by ministering to his needs. God saw first man gazing, pining, comparing and wondering why he was the only creature that was alone; he was dissatisfied and protesting silently. So, God put him to sleep because he had an excitement disorder; he was put out of commission, and an operation was performed on his musculo-skeletal-system. God adjusted that system to one rib less and used the rib He took from Adam to make Eve to compliment him. This seemed to have modified and realigned his longing. When He woke him up, he was awakened to a greater level of excitement.

When Adam recovered from his operation, he saw Eve, this brand-new creature in full view; physically, emotionally, mentally, spiritually, and visually lovely. She had filled the longing he had previously; he had not stated his case to the Creator clearly, but now, he could not control his emotions very well. He made an outburst: **"She is bone of my bone and flesh of my flesh, and he called her woman."**

In my previous book, "A Unique Passion for Healthy Marriages," I gave the definition of "Bone of My Bone and Flesh of My Flesh." **Bones** are meant to be permanent, but not eternal, meaning "I will love you forever, until death us do part."

Flesh connotes beauty, attraction, enticement; when it is activated in its fullness, then silence no longer exists. Since then, real men have never ceased to be excited. Excitement contains joy, pleasure, and the need to find delight; there will never be enough words or words that are quite ideal to define excitement in this regard.

Weakness can cause one to make serious mistakes; David was on his balcony when he saw Bathsheba bathing in a topless bathroom, and his excitement disorder kicked in. He pondered how to get her to be his wife; he decided to get her husband, Uriah, out of the way by any means necessary. So, he put him at the forefront of the battle and had him killed. Then he took her to be his wife. Having accomplished his schemes, Bathsheba bore him a child. This child did not give him the satisfaction he anticipated; instead, he experienced sleeplessness and loss of appetite, and the harmony in his music was absent.

The greatest temple in Jerusalem was built by Solomon in **957 B.C.** It took him seven years to complete; it was named after him: **"Solomon's Temple."** David was the one who designed it but his hands shed innocent blood, so he was denied the privilege of doing it. The fame forever goes to Solomon (see 2 Samuel 7:12–17).

All the credit for excitement belongs to God, the Creator, for only He can and only He could fully discern the process of excitement that Adam's imagination went through in silence. To date, men continue to seek a higher level of excitement in an effort to advance what Adam initiated when he first saw Eve.

Men will always be excited, as they were in the beginning; even so, this will continue until the end of the age. Excitement is not a man thing, it is a God thing, so let us manage our excitement in a manner that honours and glorify God; He designed us for His glory, His honour, and His praise. Everyone who does anything contrary to His design usually pays a high price.

Let us honour God, even when we are excited.

CHAPTER 7

HOW SHOULD WE CONTROL OUR EXCITEMENT

Control has always been a problem at all levels of society—with governments, organizations, institutions, and relationships—as it relates to who should have control over who and what. If the responsibility for control is not assigned fairly or left to the wishes and will of some individuals, then it can become more problematic than the need itself.

The Oxford Language defines control as follows: *"The power to influence or direct people's behavior or the course of events, to control one's anger, or to exercise restrain or directing influence over someone or something."* It also means taking responsibility for our way of life, actively making choices and decisions that aligns with values, goals and aspirations.

Regardless of how excited we become, based on our feelings about someone or something, we should ensure that our excitement aligns with our values, goals, and aspirations because there are consequences for our actions.

Excitement by itself is neither right nor wrong; depending on how one's excitement affects others and how it is controlled. It may seem normal to the excited, yet it is frowned on by others, therefore rules must first be laid down by neutral authority which should be respected by others.

In biblical terms, one's excitement must be under subjection and in harmony with one of the spiritual disciplines, **"temperance,"** which is self-control (see Galatians 5:23). It is one of the fruit of the Spirit and the fruit of the Spirit produces the character traits that are found in the nature of Christ's control; a control that is not easily obtained through personal efforts alone. Those who allow the fruit of the Spirit to grow in them will want to imitate Christ; therefore, they will love God and love people, thus fulfilling the qualities that the Spirit produces. Usually, they exhibit better traits than those who just follow the rituals but have little love in their hearts.

Self-control involves the ability to:

- exercise restraint.
- use moderation in various aspects of life.
- think with level-headedness.
- exercise willpower.
- practice self-restrain.
- practice self-discipline.

Despite one's excitement, self-control is the ability to regulate and alter one's response to undesirable or negative behavior, understand and improve one's image both in society and in the kingdom of God.

God's commandments are a matter of life and death.

"In that I command thee this day to love the Lord thy God, to walk in his ways, and to keep his commandments and his statutes and his judgments, that thou mayest live and multiply:

and the Lord thy God shall bless thee in the land whither thou goest to possess it." (Deuteronomy 30:19 – KJV).

Let us examine Genesis 2:17. God warned Adam in the Garden of Eden that if he ate from the tree of the knowledge of good and evil, he would surely die; therefore, death began on the very day he ate from it. Adam and Eve played the blame game instead of taking responsibility for what they had done, but that is no way to escape the penalty of our actions. Blaming each other is no way to escape our guilt, nor does it lead to salvation. The only way to escape our guilt is to accept that we have done wrong, seek God's forgiveness, and turn away from the error of the past to a new way with Jesus Christ, who is the way, the truth, and the life.

To illustrate, I will use four of the many examples in scriptures: one from the Old Testament and three from the New Testament:

1. **Genesis 39:1-23** tells the story of how God blessed Joseph after he was sold by his brothers to some Egyptian traders. When he settled in Egypt, the Egyptian authorities discovered his ability and giftedness as a dreamer and an interpreter of dreams; this led to his rise from a slave to prominence in Potiphar's household. He was promoted to the rank of a ruler. Potiphar gave him many responsibilities and privileges. Potiphar's wife got excited about Joseph. The Life Application Bible Commentary states that Joseph was well built and handsome, Mrs. Potiphar took notice of him, and she put her admiration and excitement into action and she lost her ability to control her excitement. **Verse 7** states she attempted to seduce Joseph to lie with her, but he resisted. Days after, she grabbed him and said, "Come lie with me." When Joseph refused and resisted her again, she

raised an alarm then lied on him. In this case, the authorities accepted her lies, so Joseph was imprisoned.

The action of Potiphar's wife teaches us that negative excitement embodies determination, falsehood, deception and sedition. It compares and contrasts two types of control:

1. A negative control-disorder by Mrs. Potiphar.
2. A positive-control by Joseph.

It is clear here that regardless of how excited one gets, self-control should override and subdue our excitement because excitement comes with responsibility.

2. **Matthew 5:2: "But I tell you that anyone who looks at a woman lustfully has already committed adultery with her in his heart." (LAB).** First man Adam's excitement declared some pertinent and lawful positions when he said, *"She is now bone of my bone, and flesh of my flesh."* This speaks to ownership, declaring she is lawfully his. The excitement of a husband toward his wife, and vice-versa, is never classified as lust because the discourse in 1 Corinthians 7:4 declares that the wife has no power over her own body, but the husband; likewise also the husband hath no power over his own body, but the wife.

3. Mark 7:14-23 says the center of a man's life is his heart. **"There is nothing from without a man, that entering into him can defile him: but the things which come out of him, those are they that defile the man." (Mark 7:15).** Therefore, we must keep our hearts with diligence because things from outside enters the belly and not the heart; our

excitements are driven from our hearts. So, once our hearts are clean, then our excitements will be clean also. Clearly, our senses can influence the state of our hearts, depending on what we read, watch, listen, taste and touch. Mark 7:20-23 puts it this way, **"An evil action begins with a single thought." (NAB).** Allowing our minds to dwell on lust, envy, hatred, or revenge will lead to sin; do not defile yourself by focusing on evil. Instead follow Paul's advice in Philippians 4:8 and think about what is true, noble, right, pure, lovely and admirable.

4. **Luke 11:4: "Forgive us our sins, for we also forgive everyone who sins against us. And lead us not into temptation." (NIV).** This model prayer demonstrates that Jesus relied on His Father for sustenance; first, He praised God, and then He made His request. We ought to rely entirely on God to grant us our requests, but we must first praise Him before we ask. We need to control our excitement.

Let us rely on Him for the help we need.

Our excitement and self-control management, from a Biblical perspective as outlined by ***"Wisdomonline.org"*** divides self-control in **three** ways: renew, guard and pray. It instructs faith in God as the most important way to control our excitement.

1. **Renew**: **Romans 12:2: "...be transformed by the renewing of your mind..." (NASB).** Study God's Word regularly to gain wisdom and understanding, which can help us to exercise self-control.

2. **Guard: Proverbs 13:3: "He that keepeth his mouth keepeth his life: but he that openeth wide his lips shall have destruction." (KJV).** Exercise self-control in your speech, refraining from gossip, anger, or hurtful words.

3. **Pray:** (see 1 Corinthians 10:13). Seek God's help through prayer; ask Him to grant you strength and self-control to resist temptation and make wise choices.

It further states that one should grow in self-control by:

- Praying for God's guidance (see Psalm 25:5).
- Pray for strength in temptation (see 1 Corinthians 10:14).
- Pray for control over our speech (see Psalm 141:3).
- Pray for patience (see Galatians 5:22-23).
- Pray for wisdom in our decision-making (see James 1:5).
- Pray for contentment (see 1 Timothy 6:6).
- Pray for gratitude (see 1 Thessalonians 5:18).
- Pray for control over desires (see 1 Corinthians 9:27).
- Pray for humility (see Philippians 2:3).
- Pray for a renewed mind (see Romans 12:2).

It is universally accepted that we are unable to properly control our excitement by ourselves; although it is recommended that we cultivate self-control, we are instructed to do the following: *"The best way to control our excitement and self-control is to rely on the Holy Spirit. He can get and keep us in alignment with His instructions."*

CHAPTER 8

TYPES OF SELF-CONTROL

There are **four** distinct types of self-control and ways to master them from a Biblical perspective, according to *Wisdominternationalonlne.org.* They involve physical movements, emotions, concentration, and impulse. There are also six subscales or elements of self-control: impulsiveness, risk-seeking, self-centeredness, preference for simple tasks, and volatile temper. The best example to follow regarding these types of self-control method is Jesus. All other persons had failures of some sort; Jesus is undoubtedly, our perfect example.

The four Types of self-control:

1. **Physical movements:** The ability to manage how the body moves and when.
2. **Emotions:** Excitement, feeling, reaction and sentiment toward a person.
3. **Concentration:** The attention or meditation on a particular matter.
4. **Impulse:** Unpredictable behavior or overacting when upset.

Six subscales or elements of self-control:

1. **Impulsiveness:** Suddenness, recklessness, or hastiness in one's action.
2. **Risk seeking:** Engaging in hazardous activities by one's choice.
3. **Preference for simple task:** Favouritism or partiality of action.
4. **Self-centeredness:** Focusing on self only while ignoring the involvement of others.
5. **Preference for simple task:** Favouritism, partiality, or fondness for one more than others.
6. **Volatile temper.** Hot-blooded, unstable, impulsive, fickle, unpredictable.

Self-control, as defined by **PSYCHOLOGS,** is as follows: *"It is the ability to control oneself, or the ability to control or manage one's impulse, emotion, or behavior toward reaching their goals. It also includes the capacity of an individual to surpass one's **tempting desires** over their regulation for the sake of one's long-term goal."*

During the Garden of Eden saga, Adam and Eve certainly did not have sufficient impulse control. Impulse control refers to the resistance against immediate desires, the urge to make a more thoughtful decision, or the tendency to delay gratification. Their "task-related control was derailed," so they obeyed the serpent's temptation, ate the fruit, and were expelled from the garden.

Proverbs 16:32 speaks of self-control regarding one's temper, in conflict, success in business, and how one's home life can be ruined by a person who loses control of his temper. Losing control may also cause one to forfeit what he wants most.

Jesus, the master self-controller, was tempted three times by the devil in the wilderness (see Matthew 4:1-11).

First Temptation: For Him to turn stones into bread; Jesus rebuked him.

Second Temptation: For Him to throw Himself down from the temple.

Third Temptation: For Jesus to fall down and worship him.

On all three occasions, Jesus neither showed excitement nor lost self-control. Once we follow His example, we are more than conquerors; after Jesus refused the devil's enticement, he left Him. It is clear that we can refuse to get excited when there are negative conditions because Jesus said He will deliver us from all evil.

Satan excited Adam and Eve earlier; then he had a try at Jesus, even though he knew the character of Jesus before he was cast out of heaven, but he still made an attempt. Satan won the first Adam, but he could not win the second Adam. Jesus is our hope, our example, and the one we use as our benchmark.

CHAPTER 9

MAN'S EXCITED HEART AND SELF CONTROL

Matthew 12:35 says, "A good man out of the good treasure of his heart, bring forth good things: and an evil man out of the evil treasure bringeth forth evil things." (KJV).** Therefore, the state of one's heart will determine the type of excitement that one exhibits.

Several people can watch an event or listen to the same message simultaneously, yet they all react differently because their reaction and excitement levels fall within different ranges; some people become easily excited.

My research reveals a diverse range of things that excite people at varying levels.

List of excitements:

1. When a father sees his newborn baby.
2. A father hearing his baby's heart-beat.
3. Hearing the word YES when you pop the big question.
4. When a young lady is spoken for who fears how her parents will react.
5. When one is selected for promotion over their very strong competitors.
6. Getting your first set of keys for your own home.

55

7. Winning a national competition.
8. Owning and driving home your brand-new car.
9. Receiving a full scholarship to a university.
10. Winning a trip to the largest hotel in the world.
11. Nominated as an administrator over your colleague.
12. Being told: 'You are the most beautiful woman in the world.'
13. Being told: 'You are the most handsome man ever.'
14. On getting exam results with the highest GPA in their class.
15. Receiving a miracle for a medical condition.
16. When Adam first saw Eve!

In Theological terms, the heart is referred to as the core of a person's inner self and the center of their life; it is the source of thoughts, passion and decisions. The *Vines Expository Dictionary of Biblical Words* states that, *"it is the seat of emotions, knowledge and wisdom; knowledge that can be used by man himself...and is considered as the seat of conscience and moral character."*

Each person has a responsibility to keep his or her heart in good condition in order to control their excitement. **Deuteronomy 6:5-6** says, **"And thou shalt love the Lord thy God with all thine heart, and with all thy soul, and with all thy might. And these words, which I command thee this day, shall be in thine heart:" (KJV).** The way we love, how we love, and the sincerity with which we love are influenced by the heart; the focus should be on the condition of the heart because it will determine the type of excitement one exhibits and also ensure a positive outcome.

"A good tree cannot bring forth evil fruit, neither can a corrupt tree bring forth good fruit." (Matthew 7:18 – KJV).

"For every tree is known by his own fruit. For of thorns men do not gather figs, nor of a bramble bush gather they grapes." (Luke 6:44 – KJV).

No amount of fright nor excitement will make a person deliver what is not stored in the heart, for out of the abundance of the heart the mouth speaketh (see Luke 6:45).

"Blessed are the pure in heart: for they shall see God." (Matthew 5:8 – KJV).

Let us ask God to help us be moderate in the way our hearts excite us, so that we do not become overly excited and do things that we will regret or pay for at a high price. The first man, Adam, sinned, and death was passed on to all humanity. Therefore, everything we do in life affects others in one way or another, whether it is today or tomorrow. No man is an island; no man stands alone; each man is my brother; each man is my friend.

CHAPTER 10

FIG LEAVES OR ANIMAL SKIN?

Knowledge can become a hindrance instead of a help to man when we do not control our excitement and disobey the rules of life. Genesis 3:5-7 puts it this way: although Adam and Eve were living together, and although Adam became excited the first time he saw her, they were okay until they disobeyed God's instruction. Disobedience is a sin. After they disobeyed God, their knowledge became a problem to them; they knew now that they were naked and attempted to cover themselves and hide from God.

Adam and Eve sewed fig leaves together and made themselves aprons in an attempt to hide from God, but can we really hide from God? Is there a place where God is not, or is there a time when His eyes are not open? Certainly not! There is no reason to hide if one is living in obedience to God's instruction; neither should guilt push us away from the presence of God. God instructed Adam and Eve not to eat from the tree in the middle of Garden. It was the tree of knowledge of good and evil (see Genesis 2:17). The other was the tree of life (see Genesis 3:22). God turned Adam away from the garden because his excitement for his wife influenced him to disobey God. Perhaps she would further influence him to eat from the tree of life as well.

The tree of life that was in the midst of the garden, in the region of the tree of the knowledge of good and evil that God removed Adam from, were both close to the river where they got their supply from (see Revelation 22:2). The tree of life brought forth twelve manners of fruit, and yielded them every month. God certainly has His plan for humanity, and all it takes is obedience to His instruction; once we obey His commands, then all will be well.

Hiding from God is totally impossible. David tried it, and it did not work for him.

"Yea, the darkness hideth not from thee; but the night shineth as the day: the darkness and the light are both alike to thee." (Psalm 139:12 - KJV).

In Genesis 3:6-7, after Adam and Eve ate the forbidden fruit and later found out that they were naked, they sewed fig leaves together and covered themselves in an effort to hide from God, but when God went to them, they were still exposed. Matthew Henry' Commentary says: *"Fig leaves will soon wither then fall, and they would be exposed again."* **Genesis 3:21** says, **"the Lord God make coats of skins, and clothed them." (KJV).** The Creator covered them, before He sent them away from the garden.

Note, however, that there could be no animal skin to cover them without the shedding of blood, which is symbolic of the account given in Matthew 26:28, which states that there is no remission of sin without the shedding of Jesus' blood. Therefore, regardless of man's efforts or how sophisticated or extensive they are, they are definitely not enough to remove the stain and guilt of sin and its punishment from the guilty sinner. Only God, through the shedding of His blood, can wash our sins away.

Satan deceived Eve by telling her that if she ate the forbidden fruit she was told not to eat, she would not die. Instead, he said her eyes would be opened and she would be as wise as gods, knowing good and evil (see Genesis 3:1-6). Satan wanted to get to Adam; he realized that the easier way to reach him was through his wife, Eve. Satan used that as bait to cover the hook, so she did not see it, and thereafter, she was caught. Adam was caught in the same trap as Eve; due to her excitement and influence on him, he ate the forbidden fruit also.

The argument that Satan introduced to Eve about being wise as gods, her eyes being opened, and she would not surely die excited her. It made her anticipate intellectual delights, open eyes, and no death for her, but to her disappointment, her excitement caused her and her husband to be expelled from the lovely Garden of Eden to a place in another garden that would produce thorns and thistles and would generate sweat to Adam's face (see Genesis 3:18). It was also declared that Eve's conception and childbearing process would have multiple sorrows and she would be in subjection to her husband (see Genesis 3:16).

CHAPTER 11

WHY DO WE COVER OURSELVES TODAY?

The first man and the first woman covered themselves with aprons made of fig leaves to hide their shame, but it was ultimately inadequate. God did not approve of their choice of covering, the reason they gave for the design, or the use of their coverings. He did not just remove it and leave them in their nakedness. Rather, He designed a different type of covering for both of them; then He covered them with a more durable type of covering. When they were created, they were naked, but it was okay. They were created as a specimen of their Creator, and no shame was involved. They were like little children until they got rude and disobeyed God's instructions.

The Creator tolerated the attempted modesty of Adam and Eve and their efforts to cover themselves. He knew that was the best they could have done in their humanness and in light of their circumstances and the resources available to them; such as adequate time to hide, a more secluded place to hide, and the wisdom to know that man cannot hide from God. God is omnipresent and omniscient; He also shows us to always resort to the best standards, and never to resort to convenience or the availability of unnecessary coverings, but to strive to prevent the need to have to hide. The best way is to prevent mistakes, rather than having them to correct.

Adam and Eve used fig leaves as their covering. Let us learn from their mistake; it was done in an effort to cover their shame; so we are to cover ourselves properly in order to prevent shameful involvements or for others to be ashamed of us. Modesty is restraining oneself from being looked at with disdain by how we dress, speak, or conduct ourselves, especially in public places.

Look carefully; Adam and Eve had to hide twice for committing sin and disobeying once.

1. They hid themselves with fig leaves.
2. They hid at one of the hideaways in the garden.

On both occasions they were found thinking they were covered and hidden, but they later realized that the fig leaves were not enough, nor was the garden a safe hiding place. Can men hide from God? It is very clear that, even though the Creator tolerated them in the Garden for a short while, He eventually expelled them. From that, we can learn that it may be convenient to hide, but there is nowhere to hide securely from the Creator. Let us seek to hide from all the things that we know will bring shame to our family, church fellowship, country, and ultimately, to the kingdom of God.

We are to hide from those who will seek to influence us to do wrong or to be engaged in the company of wrongdoers of any kind. **2 Corinthians 6:17** says: **"Wherefore come out from among them, and be ye separate, saith the Lord, and touch not the unclean thing; and I will receive you."(KJV).** The LAB commentary suggests, *"Separation from the world involves more than keeping our distance from sinners; it means staying close to God. It also involves more than avoiding entertainment that leads to sin; it extends to how we spend our time and money. There is no* *way to separate ourselves totally from all sinful influences. Nevertheless we are to resist the world around us, without either giving up or giving in."*

We are to make a clean break from our past by giving ourselves totally to God; in doing so, there will be no need to hide. Let us do all we can to avoid a similar fate like that of Adam and Eve.

There are standards in every family, organization, country, or province, and, in most cases, these standards are governed by policies, procedures, and cultures. There are also privacy and modesty standards by which people are governed; if these standards are violated, there are usually consequences for doing so. Let us cover ourselves to prevent all forms of shame.

SECTION 3

CHAPTER 12

CAN ONE BE NAKED, EXCITED, AND STILL BE MORALLY SOUND?

In the beginning, when God created Adam, he remained naked yet it was okay; after He created Eve, she too was naked and yet good. Before they disobeyed God's instruction, they were both naked and remained morally sound (see Genesis 2:25). It was not until they were beguiled by the serpent that they decided it was not okay, then they discovered the need to cover themselves and the need to hide (see Genesis 3:7).

Babies do not know the difference between nakedness and being clothed because they are innocent. When their brains are developed and they start to mature, then they begin to make that distinction. The wise man Solomon said, **"To every thing there is a season, and a time to every purpose under the heaven:" (Ecclesiastes 3:1 – KJV).**

There are some persons who get excited and inspired while they are in their bathrooms; naked. They sing, recite, preach, and compose songs and prayers; obviously, they will cover themselves before leaving the bathroom once they suspect they will be seen by others. We could do our best in those special moments, but one still needs to know that there are boundaries we should not cross by exposing ourselves to others.

The word "naked" appears eighty-six times in the Old Testament, and, most of the times it appears, it is in reference to persons being reprimanded for exposing themselves or as a punishment for wrongdoing. There are occasions where things that were done in secret were brought to light by others, and as a consequence, they were forcefully uncovered and left naked.

There are examples of persons who had bad experiences and were humiliated for their actions:

1.	Adam and Eve in the Garden of Eden.	**Genesis 3:7**
2.	Noah got drunk and uncovered himself in his tent; two of his sons saw his nakedness and were ashamed.	**Genesis 9:20-26**
3.	The Israelites in the temple space were told to dress discretely and not to expose themselves.	**Exodus 20:26**
4.	After Saul was rejected as king, he prophesied naked all day and night in the presence of Samuel the prophet.	**1 Samuel 19:18-24**
5.	The Egyptian captive and the Cushite exiles were naked and barefooted with their buttocks uncovered.	**Isaiah 20:4**
6.	Persons who fill themselves with their own glory will be filled with disgrace and nakedness, instead of being honoured.	**Habakkuk 2:16**

7.	Paul used nakedness as a condition that can cause people to separate themselves from the love of God; he vowed he would not be separated.	**Romans 8:33-38**
8.	Israelite men love to wear their beards. Hunun, the son of Nahash the Amorite, instructed his men to forcefully shave the Israelites and strip them half-naked to humiliate and embarrass them.	**1 Chronicles 19:4-5**
9.	Isaiah was stripped and left barefooted for three years; it was a humiliating experience because Judah put their trust in foreign governments against the will of God.	**Isaiah 20:2-3**
10.	Nakedness is associated with destitution, drunkenness, or when it is as a result of a robbery.	**Luke 10:30, Acts 19:16, and James 2:15**

Many positive things are being done by persons every day while they are naked. The wise man Solomon said in **Ecclesiastes 3:1, "To everything there is a season, and a time to every purpose under the heaven." (KJV).** To do some surgeries in an operating theatre, the patient has to be stripped naked. Therefore, to correct some ills, the process demands that nakedness is the state in which the correction must be done.

It is safe to say we can do some great and outstanding things while being naked. It is also safe to say that our garments can be a hindrance to some positive processes. We must get naked in order to get clean physically, be stripped naked in order to do some medical procedures, strip off old garments in order to get new ones, and to be cleansed spiritually, we have to lay aside the garments that are stained with sin; and the list goes on.

Let us think positively!

CHAPTER 13

WHAT HAPPENS IF A THOUSAND MEN SEE A WOMAN?

There are bound to be thousands of excitements towards a woman if a thousand men see her, and the excitement will manifest in various ways.

It is almost a mystery how men react to women, especially those who are unusual because there are no manuals for each man's masculine response; each one tends to act according to his own individuality.

Some men can be shy, bold, expressive, outgoing, reserved, particularly nervous, emotional, or overly reactive, but all can become excited whenever they are in the presence of a woman. Presumably, it works the same way when women are in the presence of men. A man's excitement may kick in towards a woman in a particular way, while another man's excitement towards the same woman may kick in quite differently, but for sure, each man's awareness gets alerted every time they see a woman. This is so whether she is:

- Black, white or yellow.
- Fluffy, slim or moderate.
- Married, single or divorced.
- Beautiful, moderate or difficult to look at.

- Well-dressed or she hardly leaves anything for the imagination.
- Whether she is a Christian or a non-Christian.

Gender difference knows no bounds.

There is a reason why Jesus gave the instruction regarding inward purity, impurity, lust, chastity, and evil imagination. He is the ultimate authority on the human body.

Matthew 5:28, "But I say unto you, That whosoever looketh on a woman to lust after her hath committed adultery with her already in his heart." (KJV).

The desire of a husband for his wife does not fall in the category of lust because his wife's body is his; likewise his body is hers. The two have become one in the bond of marriage; a legal partner has the right to be excited about their partner at any time.

Matthew 5:28 LAB commentary says, *"Some may think that if lustful thoughts are sin, then why shouldn't a person just go-a-head and carry out the lustful actions too?"* Acting out lustful desires are harmful in many ways:

1. It causes people to make excuse for sin, rather than to stop sinning.
2. It destroys marriages.
3. It is a deliberate rebellion against God's Word.
4. It always hurt someone else in addition to the sinner.

Desires should not be acted out; a sinful action is more dangerous than a sinful desire. Nevertheless, sinful desires are just as damaging to righteousness if left unchecked. Where doubts and guilt are detected and corrected, the sin of omission is enacted. Wrong desires will result in wrong actions and turn people away from God.

It further states that Jesus is not condemning our natural interest in the opposite sex or even having healthy sexual desires, but the deliberate and repeated filling of one's mind with fantasies that would be evil if acted out; those are the things we are to hide from. It further states that God's grace is the greatest covering for humanity; we should cover ourselves with His grace and not try to hide from Him. Rather, let us hide ourselves in Him, who undoubtedly is the greatest hiding place of all.

The thought, *"Behaviour is learnt"* is a well-accepted one and comes into play frequently when we see others do things that catch our attention. If we admire those persons or things and cherish them long enough, then we may develop a desire for them. ***The Hugs Bible for Women*** speaks of ***"The Vanity of Pleasure."***

"And whatsoever mine eyes desired I kept not from them, I withheld not my heart from any joy; for my heart rejoiced in all my labour: and this was my portion of all my labour. Then I looked on all the works that my hands had wrought, and on the labour that I had laboured to do: and, behold, all was vanity and vexation of spirit, and there was no profit under the sun." (Ecclesiastes 2:10-11 – KJV).

The wise man Solomon said in **Ecclesiastes 1:2-3, "Vanity of vanities, saith the Preacher, vanity of vanities; all is vanity. What profit hath a man of all his labour which he taketh under the sun?" (KJV).**

CHAPTER 14

DO NOT ALLOW EXCITEMENT TO TRIGGER WRONG DECISIONS

"The light of the body is the eye: if therefore thine eye be single, thy whole body shall be full of light. But if thine eye be evil, thy whole body shall be full of darkness. If therefore the light that is in thee be darkness, how great is that darkness!" (Matthew 6:22-23 – KJV).

Sight goes beyond the ordinary and is much deeper than just physical eyesight; it drives the perception method and is one of the characteristics of faith. Often, we make wrong decisions based on a single glance of the eye, without perceiving the deeper issues, and, most importantly, by not relying on God to guide our steps.

We make impulsive decisions when the things we see fill our eyes, and we may get excited. Then, in our excitement, we make major decisions that carry a high price and can affect the following:

1. Business
2. Relationships
3. Marriages
4. Job opportunities
5. Health
6. Safety

7. Security
8. Our faith

"I said in my haste, All men are liars." (Psalm 116:11 – KJV).

"I said in my haste, all men are deceitful and liars." (Psalm 116:11 – AMPC).

"Yes, even when I was upset and said, "There is no one I can trust!" (Psalm 116:11 – ERV).

The Psalmist David spoke rashly about men who told him he would recover when he had his near-death experience. He cried to the Lord because he was frightened, sad, and lost hope completely; they told him he would recover, and he said they were liars. At that point, he saw nothing but hopelessness:

"The lord protects the simple and the childlike; I was facing death, and then He saved me, now I can relax for the Lord has done this wonderful miracle for me. He has saved me from death, my eyes from tears, my feet from stumbling. I shall live! Yes, in His presence, here on earth." (Psalm 116:6-9 – TLB).

In Psalm 116:10-13, David said later, **"In my discouragement, I thought, they were all liars, when they say I would recover, but now, What can I offer to Jehovah for all that He has done for me. I will bring Him an offering of wine and praise His name for saving me." (TLB).**

We are prone to similar mistakes as David; hasty actions can jeopardize major decisions in our lives. Therefore, we must subject our excitement to the will of God in everything in order not to have regrets.

Ecclesiastes 5:2 states, **"Be not rash with thy mouth, and let not thine heart be hasty to utter anything before God: For God is in heaven, and thou upon earth: therefore, let thy words be few." (KJV).**

The **Ecclesiastes 5:2 LAB commentary** says, *"Solomon warns his readers about making foolish vows. Promise-making vows was a serious matter in the Israelite culture; they were voluntary but once made were unbreakable."* In today's world, and especially for Christians, we are to make our words our bond. Let us speak only the things that we believe and make our words our bond.

CHAPTER 15

BE CAREFUL NOT TO OVEREXCITE OTHERS BY OUR DISPOSITION AND DRESSING

Most people get excited by what they see; then they want to hear more about it and explore the possibilities of touching, smelling, and tasting until their five basic senses are engaged as part of the assessment process. Before our sensory systems become fully activated or overexcited, if we make our decisions based on how the senses function, then we are prone to making foolish decisions. When we act on impulse, we usually have regrets. We need to depend on God to order our steps instead of regretting some of the decisions we make and paying a high price; in some cases, we may have to continue paying for a lifetime. Let us learn that there is more to life than a look of the eye.

There is a degree of pretense in everyone, putting our best foot forward, which is not altogether bad but must be governed by the wisdom that comes from God. This wisdom will cause us to make every effort to measure up to the standard by which we present ourselves so that we are not classified as fake or a pretender.

The hearts of men can be troubled, and there are many reasons why this is so. The heart is the seat of man's affection or the real person because our deeds come from the heart. A heart can contain impurity, bondage, sadness, fear and hatred. The things mentioned previously can prevent our happiness, freedom, purity, love, and

81

peace; therefore, it is important that we keep ourselves with diligence. **Jeremiah 17:9** says, **"The heart is deceitful above all things, and desperately wicked: who can know it?" (KJV).** We know that persons will do things they know are wrong, then try to justify their deeds and may even attempt to twist the hand of the righteous to accept their way of life.

From time to time, and in various ways, people engage in provocative actions to excite and seduce others into adopting their styles and behavior; they may even go so far as to add sweeteners to their actions to attract others. There are so many ways in which one can excite others; here are some examples:

1. By provocative dressing.
2. By provocative behaviors.
3. Giving exaggerated respect.
4. Direct and prolonged eye contact with smiles.
5. Winking, blinking, and other eye movements.
6. Leading several persons along at the same time.
7. Showing great interest.
8. Using a suggestive tone of voice.
9. Being extraordinarily generous.
10. Being extraordinarily helpful.
11. Being overly available.

Overexcitement can make a person vulnerable, causing them to make mistakes. Excitement with assertiveness is better than excitement with vulnerability, for the price of vulnerability is usually too high.

When we depend on God to provide our life partner, there are usually no regrets. He put Adam to sleep, performed that special operation, and then presented Eve to him. We can trust Him to provide, present to us, and excite us with our life's partner. We can learn from Adam's experience; he had a longing, but he had no choice. We, on the other hand, have our longing, and we have choices. **Psalm 37:23** says, **"The steps of a good man are ordered by the Lord: and he delighteth in his ways." (KJV).** Psalm 37:23 LAB commentary puts it this way: *"The person in whom God delights is one who follows Him, trust Him, and tries to do His will; God watches over and makes firm every step that a person takes. If you would like to have God direct your way, then seek His advice before you step out."*

Obviously, we are to commit our excitement to the will of God; in so doing, we will not overexcite anyone, nor will anyone overexcite us. Our pursuit of intimate excitement should always be directed toward one end, and that is "the one-flesh union." It was never the will of God for an "anything-goes" situation. He wants an undefiled bed.

Hebrews 13:4 says, **"Marriage is honourable in all, and the bed undefiled, but whoremonger and adulterers God will judge." (KJV).** Hebrews 13:4 LAB commentary says, *"Real love for others produces tangible actions: kindness to strangers, respect for marriage vows, contentment with what you have, make sure that your love runs deep enough to affect your hospitality, empathy, fidelity and contentment."*

Luke 12:47-48 speaks of judgement according to privilege: **"And that servant, which knew his lord's will, and prepared not himself, neither did according to his will, shall be beaten with many stripes. But he that knew not, and did commit things worthy of stripes, shall be beaten with few stripes. For unto**

whomsoever much is given, of him shall be much required: and to whom men have committed much, of him they will ask the more." (KJV).

Therefore, we know that the Lord delights not in negative excitement, so we are to do only those things in which He delights.

CONCLUSION

From creation until now, men have not ceased to be excited. Despite learning from Adam's mistake and the consequences he suffered for his act of disobedience, excitement remains a permanent feature of mankind. Regarding the Ancient Greek Philosopher Heraclitus' famous philosophy that "the only thing in life that is constant is change," I have observed changes in the extent of human excitement behavior, but not in the behavior itself. There is a continuous search for a greater level of excitement as mankind drives for happiness and more excitement. **Heraclitus** further stated that he believed that the world is in a state of perpetual change, where nothing remains static or permanent. Hence, the search for a higher dimension of excitement. Men have always wanted more. The categories of **excitement** are as follows:

- Positive excitement.
- Comparative excitement.
- Superlative excitement.

Even though the consequences remain constant, the extent to which one bears it may differ in proportionality.

Below are some listed Biblical points:

1. **"For his sake, was the ground cursed" (see Genesis 3:17).**

2. "In sorrow he would eat of the ground, for the rest of his life" (see Genesis 3:17).

3. "The ground would bring forth thistle" (see Genesis 3:18).

4. "He shall eat the herb of the field" (see Genesis 3:18).

5. "He would eat bread by the sweat of his face, for his entire life" (see Genesis 3:19).

6. "Man shall return to the dust from whence he came" (see Genesis 3:19).

7. Adam and Eve were expelled from paradise (see Genesis 3:23-24).

Man has not changed their excitement pattern since creation. Every time a man sees a woman, excitement kicks in, even though the consequences meted out to both Adam and Eve for their excitement and disobedience were so great. It led to their expulsion; they were removed from their perfect home in the garden, and a restriction was placed around it to prevent them from returning to the paradise they previously enjoyed. In theological terms, excitement survived all seven dispensations and all three eras, *according to google.com/sear.*

Dispensations:

1.	Innocence	Genesis 1:28-30
2.	Conscience	Genesis 3:8 and 3:23-24
3.	Human Government	Genesis 8:22

4. Promise	Genesis 12:1, Exodus 19:25
5. Law	Exodus 19-23
6. Grace	Luke 22:20
7. The Millennial Kingdom of Christ	Revelation 20:11-14, Chapters 21 and 22

Eras:

1. The Ancient Period: 3600 BC – 500 AD.
2. The Middle Ages or Medieval: 500 AD. – 1500 AD.
3. Modern Era: 1500 AD – Present.

Adam and Eve traded their lives of joy, ease, and comfort for a short moment of excitement. They took instructions from the wrong source and ate from the forbidden tree, which God instructed them not to eat from. Short moments of pleasure can lead to a lifetime of regret and sorrow. Therefore, we should learn to evaluate the risks associated with our actions in moments of great excitement, temptation, and freedom.

Then, there comes the reality; freedom comes with responsibility. When the assessment and reflections are complete and the conclusion is drawn, then come these words: *"It is too late now."* Usually, it is then that we realize the dreams we chased have turned into nightmares, and the pursuit of excitement and happiness has ruined our future, security, hopes, and peace and also led to nonconformity with organizational rules. We end up eating the sour grapes and set our children's teeth on edge.

On many occasions, when we have regrets, we conclude that if we had known then what we know now, we would order our lives differently.

Whether we are excited a thousand times or we are not excited all remains a matter of choice, but remember that **choice comes with responsibility.**

Uncle Sam's parting words to me were always: "Boy, be good! But if you cannot be good, be careful!

OTHER BOOKS BY THE AUTHOR

What is marriage? What does marriage entail, and is it meant to be long-term? This book details the answers to these questions and more. Written in the form of an interview, these questions are addressed, outlining what is expected in a marriage.

We need to think of how life will be with a partner, how to overcome challenges, and how to resolve conflicts and misunderstandings. This book promotes communication as the key ingredient to successful relationships and answers the question of whether or not marriage is still relevant.

William was born in the district of Marlie Hill, Manchester. He spent his formative years there. He received his early education at the Marlie Hill Elementary School. He later migrated to May Pen, Clarendon in 1977 and currently resides in Mineral Heights.

He has been married to Arlene since September 02, 1978, and the union produced two children.

Researched and compiled by Rev. William D. Hutchinson for the laity and established and potential leaders on social issues for all sectors of society.

William is a Christian and is actively involved in serving in the following capacities: Administrative Assistant to the National Bishop, with specific responsibility for Clarendon South COGOP, which consists of twenty-three churches. He pastors the Bustamante Highway and Free Town churches. He has served in the following churches: Hayes, Palmers Cross, Rocky Point, Longville, Old Monymusk, and Free Town COGOP previously, and as interim pastor for Savannah Cross, Mount Airy, Foga Road, and Mt.

Providence COGOP. He is also serving on four COGOP National Boards.

He is a Justice of The Peace, a Marriage Officer since 1998, author, and a volunteer in the Clarendon Chapter of the Jamaica Red Cross Society.

He holds a Master of Arts in Religion and a Diploma in Christian Leadership from Gordon Conwell Theological Seminary (USA); Diploma in Practical Theology from International Seminary (USA); Diploma in Practical English from International Correspondence School (USA); Diploma in Religious Education from Bible Training Institute COGOP (Kingston, Jamaica); Diploma in Production and Operations Management from IMP (Now University of the Caribbean); Diploma in Automotive and Diesel Mechanics from National Technical School (NTS) California, USA.

In addition, he holds numerous certificates and licenses from other leading and recognized organizations in Jamaica and abroad, which include the College of Insurance and Professionals (Kingston, Jamaica), the American College of Insurance and Professionals (USA), Jamaica Institute of Management (JIM) Kingston, Jamaica, the Job Bank (Kingston, Jamaica), the Marriage Unit (Ministry of Justice) and the Church Of God Of Prophecy (Cleveland, Tennessee, USA).

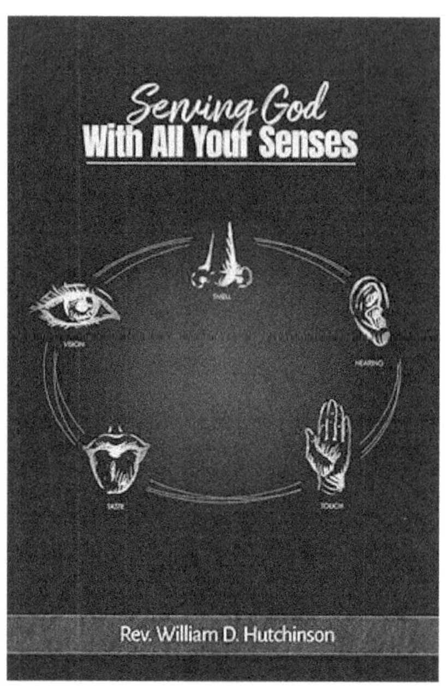

Engaging with God becomes a profound experience when we employ all our senses in worship. By immersing ourselves fully, we elevate the quality of service, not only to Him but also to others. In the realm of focused devotion, our impact transcends mere effort, profoundly benefiting both our organizations and the bonds of fellowship.

Reflecting on Romans 12:01 (NIV) where we are urged, "in view of God's mercy, to offer your bodies as a living sacrifice, holy and pleasing to God—this is your true and proper worship," we discover that true worship emerges when we invest all our senses. Achieving this level of devotion represents the pinnacle of our spiritual journey, a goal that resonates deeply within us all. So, let us embark on this sacred endeavor with the entirety of our senses, enriching our worship and deepening our connection with God.

ABOUT THE AUTHOR

William D. Hutchinson is a husband of over forty-six years, a father of two children, and a grandfather of five grandchildren. He is a pastor, a marriage officer, a counselor, a church administrator, a national worker of COGOP, a Justice of the Peace, an Executive Member of the Clarendon Branch of the Jamaica Red Cross Society, and an author of four other books: "Autobiography and Pictorials of a Fulfilled Life." "A Unique Passion for Healthy Marriages," "A Compilation of Inspired Sermons For the Laity Established and Potential Leaders On Social Issues For All Sectors Of Society," and "Serving God With All Your Senses." He has over 41 years of pastoral ministry experience, and enjoys a good relationship with his colleagues and pastorates. He lives by the motto: *"Whatever is worth doing, is worth doing well."*